Drama for Students, Volume 4

Staff

Editorial: David M. Galens, *Editor*. Terry Browne, Christopher Busiel, Clare Cross, John Fiero, David M. Galens, Carole Hamilton, D. L. Kellett, Erika Kreger, Sheri Metzger, Daniel Moran, Terry Nienhuis, Arnold Schmidt, William P. Wiles, Etta Worthington, *Entry Writers*. Elizabeth Cranston, Catherine V. Donaldson, Kathleen J. Edgar, Jennifer Gariepy, Dwayne D. Hayes, Joshua Kondek, Tom Ligotti, Scot Peacock, Patti Tippett, Pam Zuber, *Contributing Editors*. James Draper, *Managing Editor*. Diane Telgen, *"For Students" Line Coordinator*. Jeffery Chapman, *Programmer/Analyst*.

Research: Victoria B. Cariappa, *Research Team Manager*. Andy Malonis, Barb McNeil, *Research Specialists*. Julia C. Daniel, Tamara C. Nott, Tracie A. Richardson, Cheryl L. Warnock, *Research Associates*. Phyllis P. Blackman, Jeffrey D. Daniels,

Corrine A. Stocker, *Research Assistants*.

Permissions: Susan M. Trosky, *Permissions Manager*. Kimberly F. *Smilay Permissions Specialist*. Steve Cusack and Kelly A. Quin, *Permissions Associates*.

Production: Mary Beth Trimper, *Production Director*. Evi Seoud, *Assistant Production Manager*. Shanna Heilveil, *Production Assistant*.

Graphic Services: Randy Bassett, *Image Database Supervisor*. Robert Duncan and Michael Logusz, *Imaging Specialists*. Pamela A. Reed, *Photography Coordinator*. Gary Leach, *Macintosh Artist*.

Product Design: Cynthia Baldwin, *Product Design Manager*. Cover Design: Michelle DiMercurio, *Art Director*. Page Design: Pamela A. E. Galbreath, *Senior Art Director*.

Copyright Notice

Since this page cannot legibly accommodate all copyright notices, the acknowledgments constitute an extension of the copyright notice.

While every effort has been made to secure permission to reprint material and to ensure the reliability of the information presented in this publication, Gale Research neither guarantees the accuracy of the data contained herein nor assumes any responsibility for errors, omissions, or discrepancies. Gale accepts no payment for listing; and inclusion in the publication of any organization, agency, institution, publication, service, or individual does not imply endorsement of the editors or publisher. Errors brought to the attention of the publisher and verified to the satisfaction of the publisher will be corrected in future editions.

This publication is a creative work fully protected by all applicable copyright laws, as well as by misappropriation, trade secret, unfair competition, and other applicable laws. The authors and editors of this work have added value to the underlying factual material herein through one or more of the following: unique and original selection, coordination, expression, arrangement, and classification of information. All rights to this publication will be vigorously defended.

Copyright © 1998
Gale Research
835 Penobscot Building
645 Griswold Detroit, MI 48226-4094

All right reserved including the right of reproduction in whole or in part in any form.

This book is printed on acid-free paper that meets the minimum requirements of American National Standard for Information Sciences—Permanence Paper for Printed Library Materials, ANSI Z39.48-1984.

ISBN 0-7876-2753-4
ISSN 1094-9232

Printed in the United States of America
10 9 8 7 6 5 4

The Importance of Being Earnest

Oscar Wilde

1895

Introduction

Oscar Wilde's most successful play, *The Importance of Being Earnest* became an instant hit when it opened in London, England, in February, 1895, running for eighty-six performances. The play has remained popular with audiences ever since, vying with Wilde's 1890 novel *The Portrait of Dorian Gray* as his most recognized work. The play proves vexing to critics, though, for it resists categorization, seeming to some merely a flimsy plot which serves as an excuse for Wilde's witty epigrams (terse, often paradoxical, sayings or catch-phrases). To others it is a penetratingly humorous and insightful social comedy.

When *Earnest* opened, Wilde was already familiar to readers for *Dorian Gray*, as well as for collections of fairy tales, stories, and literary criticism. Theatre-goers knew him for his earlier dramatic works, including three previous successes, *Lady Windermere's Fan* (1892), *A Women of No Importance* (1893), and *An Ideal Husband* (1895), as well as for his more controversial play, *Salome* (1896), which was banned in Britain for its racy (by nineteenth century standards) sexual content.

The Importance of Being Earnest has been favorably compared with William Shakespeare's comedy *Twelfth Night* and Restoration plays like Richard Brinsley Sheridan's *School for Scandal* and Oliver Goldsmith's *She Stoops to Conquer*. While it is generally acknowledged that Wilde's play owes a debt to these works, critics have contended that the playwright captures something unique about his era, reworking the late Victorian melodramas and stage romances to present a farcical, highly satiric work—though audiences generally appraise the play as simply great fun.

Tragically, as *The Importance of Being Earnest*, his fourth and most successful play, received acclaim in London, Wilde himself became embroiled in the legal actions against his homosexuality that would end his career and lead to imprisonment, bankruptcy, divorce, and exile.

Author Biography

Oscar (Fingal O'Flahertie Wills) Wilde was born on October 15 (though some sources cite October 16), 1854 (some sources cite 1856) in Dublin, Ireland, where he would spend his youth. His father was a celebrated eye and ear surgeon who was knighted by Queen Victoria for founding a hospital and writing an influential medical textbook. Wilde's mother, Jane Francesca Elgee Wilde, came to be called "Speranza," writing poems, stories, essays, and folklore meant to give hope to advocates of rights for women and Ireland.

Wilde won prizes in the classics at Portora Royal School in Ulster, and his continued success in classic studies at Dublin's Trinity College won him a scholarship to attend Magdalen College, Oxford, where he earned a B.A. In 1878, the undergraduate Wilde won the Newdigate Prize for his poem "Ravenna."

While at Oxford, the ideas of Walter Pater and John Ruskin shaped Wilde's thinking about art. He became known for flamboyance in dress (his trademark became wearing a green carnation in his lapel), collecting peacock feathers, and blue china; he came to personify the term "Dandy" used to describe men who paid excessive attention to their appearance. He also became a spokesman for Aestheticism, a belief in the supreme importance of "Art for Art's sake," without regard for its practical, ethical, or social purpose. ("The object of Art is not simple truth but complex beauty," Wilde wrote later in his 1889 essay "The Decay of Lying.") Following publication of the first volume of his *Poems* in 1881, which included "The Harlot's House" and "Impression du Matin," Wilde spent ten months giving 125 lectures throughout the United States. The Aesthetics movement and Wilde were satirized in the magazine *Punch* and in W. S. Gilbert's *Patience* (1881).

After the disappointing reception of his first play, *Vera*, in 1883, Wilde returned to Britain to spend eighteen months lecturing on "Impressions of America." In 1884, he married Constance Lloyd and began working as a reviewer and editor. *The Happy Prince and Other Tales*, a volume of fairy tales originally written for his sons appeared in 1888, followed two years later by Wilde's novel, *The Picture of Dorian Gray*.

Success eluded Wilde's second play, *The Duchess of Padua* (1891), but his subsequent theatrical efforts received increasing acclaim: *Lady Windermere's Fan* in 1892, *A Women of No Importance* in 1893, *An Ideal Husband* in 1895, and, that same year, his greatest theatrical success, *The Importance of Being Earnest*.

While in Paris, Wilde wrote *Salome* in French, but the play was refused a license for performance in England, though the 1896 Paris production starred noted actress Sara Bernhardt. An English translation of *Salome* appeared in 1894 with illustrations by famed illustrator Aubrey Beardsley and the play provided the libretto for Richard Strauss's successful 1905 opera of the same name.

Social criticism of Wilde's openly homosexual behavior (though married with children, he professed a deep passion for young men) led to the end of his career. Wilde's relationship with Lord Alfred Douglas led Douglas's father, the Marquess of Queensberry, to publicly accuse Wilde of sodomy. Encouraged by Lord Alfred, Wilde sued the Marquess for slander, losing his suit when the Marquess offered evidence of Wilde's homosexuality. Wilde refused the advice of friends to flee to the Continent and in subsequent trials was convicted of "public indecency" and sentenced to two years of hard labor. With the scandal, Wilde's plays ceased production.

Two major works written in prison were published following Wilde's release. *De Profundus* appeared in 1905, offering an apologetic confession of Wilde's conduct, while *The Ballad of Reading Gaol*, published initially in 1898, indicts England's prison system and tells of his experiences there. Upon his release, Wilde, divorced and bankrupt, adopted the name Sebastian Melmouth and moved to Paris, France, where he died in 1900.

Wilde's literary reputation enjoyed a considerable resurgence in the years following his death. He is now regarded as one of modern literature's major figures. His skill and diversity within multiple genres has earned him respect as a poet, novelist, essayist, and playwright. His works are still widely studied and his plays enjoy frequent revivals.

Plot Summary

Act One

The play opens in the fashionable London residence of Algernon Moncrieff. His friend Jack (who goes by the name "Earnest") Worthing arrives, revealing his intention to propose matrimony to Algernon's cousin Gwendolen Fairfax. In the course of their conversation, Jack admits that he is the ward to a young woman, Cecily Cardew. Also, he admits to leading a double life, stating that his "name is Earnest in town and Jack in the country." In the country, he pretends to have a brother in London named Earnest whose wicked ways necessitate frequent trips to the city to rescue him.

Algernon's aunt Lady Augusta Bracknell arrives with his cousin Gwendolen Fairfax. While Algernon and his aunt discuss the music for her next party, Jack—claiming his name is Earnest—confesses his love for Gwendolen and proposes marriage. She is delighted, because her "ideal has always been to love someone of the name Earnest." When the lovers tell Lady Bracknell their news, she responds frostily, forbidding marriage outright after learning that while Jack has an occupation—he smokes—and money, he has no lineage to boast of —in fact, he has no knowledge of his real family at all. He was discovered as an infant, abandoned in a handbag in Victoria Station.

Because Cecily seems too interested in Jack's imaginary brother, Earnest, Jack decides to "kill" him. Gwendolen informs Jack that while Lady Bracknell forbids their marriage and that she "may marry someone else, and marry often," she will retain her "eternal devotion" to him.

Act Two

July in the garden of Jack's Manor House in Hertfordshire. Miss Prism, Cecily's governess, chides her for not attending to her German lesson, as Jack has requested. Prism informs Cecily that when younger, she had written a novel. The Rector, Canon Frederick Chasuble enters, suggesting that a stroll in the garden may cure Miss Prism's headache.

She feels fine but a headache develops soon after his suggestion, and they walk off together.

Algernon arrives, and, finding Cecily alone, introduces himself as Jack's "wicked" city brother, Earnest. Cecily and Algernon (as Earnest) walk off. Prism and Chasuble return as Jack shows up unexpectedly. Hoping to end his double-life, Jack informs them that his brother Earnest has died in Paris of a "severe chill." They console him, until Cecily enters with Earnest (Algernon), who seems very much alive. Jack is bewildered, but Cecily, thinking Jack's coolness is resentment at his brother's dissipated lifestyle, insists that the "brothers" mend their relationship.

Left alone, Algernon proposes to Cecily, only to discover that—according to Cecily—they have already been engaged for three months. It seems that since Cecily heard from Jack about his wicked brother, Earnest, she fell in love with him. She entered in her diary their entire romance, complete with proposal, acceptance, break-up, and reconciliation.

Gwendolen arrives and chats with Cecily, until both women realize they are engaged to a man named Earnest. When Algernon and Jack return, their true identities—and the fact that neither of them is actually named Earnest—are revealed. As the scene ends, both men admit to having arranged for Chasuble to re-christen them with the name Earnest.

Act Three

Later the same day at the Manor house, Gwendolen and Cecily prepare to forgive the men, though they are disappointed that neither is named Earnest. Lady Bracknell arrives, in pursuit of Gwendolen. She learns from Jack that his ward Cecily is quite wealthy and therefore a desirable match for her nephew Algernon. When she hears of Miss Prism, Lady Bracknell recognizes her as a former family servant. Prism and Lady Bracknell's infant nephew had disappeared at the same time under mysterious circumstances.

Miss Prism confesses that she had left the house with her novel manuscript in one hand and the baby in the other. In her confusion, however, she had put the book in the baby carriage and the baby in the handbag at the train station. The baby, Jack, turns out to be Lady Bracknell's lost nephew and Algernon's older brother. Lady Bracknell now gives her permission for Algernon to wed Cecily, but Jack, as Cecily's guardian, refuses his permission unless Lady Bracknell consents to his marriage to Gwendolen. She does, and as the act closes, they learn that Jack was named after his father, General Earnest John Moncrieff—Earnest for short.

Characters

Algy

See Algernon Moncrieff

Lady Augusta Bracknell

Algernon's aunt and the sister of Jack's mother. She opposes Jack's marriage with her daughter Gwendolen, though relents when she learns that Jack is actually her nephew. More accurately, she wants Algernon to be able to marry the very wealthy Cecily, but that match cannot take place without Jack's permission, which he refuses to give unless Lady Bracknell approves his marriage with Gwendolen. Overall, she is realistic, hard-nosed, and an upholder of convention—though not entirely conventional herself.

Cecily Cardew

Jack's pretty, young ward, whom Algernon woos but who remains determined to marry a man named Earnest. Not quite as naive as she may appear, Cecily keeps a diary, which "is simply a very young girl's record of her own thoughts and impressions and consequently meant for publication." Tutored by Miss Prism, Cecily fails to attend to her studies and marries Algernon at the play's conclusion.

Canon Frederick Chasuble

Canon Chasuble is the rather foolish, pedantic Rector attracted to Miss Prism. Both Jack and Algernon ask Chasuble to christen them Earnest, though no christening actually takes place. As Cecily says, "He has never written a single book, so you can imagine how much he knows."

Earnest

See John Worthing

Gwendolen Fairfax

Algernon's cousin, with whom Jack—as Earnest—is in love and to whom he proposes marriage. She accepts, believing him to be Algy's friend Earnest. As she explains to Jack, her "ideal has always been to love someone of the name Earnest. There is something in that name that inspires absolute confidence." Her mother, Lady Augusta Bracknell, initially forbids their marriage, because while Jack seems an otherwise eligible bachelor, he cannot identify his parents, as he was found abandoned in a handbag. The play's end, however, establishes Jack's identity; Lady Bracknell grants permission, and the lovers are united.

Lane

The self-deprecating butler who serves Algernon in his London residence.

Merriman

The servant at Jack's country manor house in Hertfordshire.

Algernon Moncrieff

Jack (Earnest) Worthing's friend, Lady Bracknell's nephew, and Gwendolen's cousin. In order to free himself from unwanted social and family responsibilities, Algy has invented an invalid friend, Bunbury, whose ailing health frequently—and conveniently—requires Algernon's attention, enabling him to skip dinners with boring guests and tiresome relatives.

Ostentatiously cynical and constantly hungry, Algernon pretends to be Jack's brother Earnest and visits Jack's ward Cecily Cardew. He falls in love with her and proposes matrimony. Jack refuses his permission for Algernon to marry Cecily unless Lady Bracknell gives her permission for Jack to marry Gwendolen, which, at the play's end, she does. The mystery of Jack's parentage reveals that Jack and Algy are actually brothers.

Miss Laetitia Prism

Cecily's absentminded governess who is wooed by Chasuble. Formerly, while working for Lady Bracknell, she wrote a novel then lost Jack in the railway station. She "deposited the manuscript in the bassinet, and placed the baby in the handbag," which was lost in the cloak room of Victoria Station.

John Worthing

John "Jack" Worthing (Earnest) begins the play of unknown parentage, an orphaned infant found in a handbag in a cloak room at London's Victoria Station. Discovered and raised by Thomas Cardew, Jack becomes guardian of Cardew's granddaughter, Cecily. Though he calls himself Jack in the country, he identifies himself as Earnest when in the city. In order to excuse himself when he leaves for the city, he tells Cecily that he must get his wicked citified brother, Earnest, out of various scrapes. In time, Cecily becomes infatuated with this imaginary brother Earnest. By the play's end, it is revealed that Miss Prism had left Jack at the station, that Lady Bracknell's sister Mrs. Moncrieff is his mother, and that Jack is Algy's elder brother. Also, significantly, Jack, who has been named after his father General Earnest John Moncrieff, actually *is* named Earnest.

Themes

Morals and Morality

Much of *The Importance of Being Earnest's* comedy stems from the ways various characters flaunt the moral strictures of the day, without ever behaving beyond the pale of acceptable society. The use of the social lie is pervasive, sometimes carried to great lengths as when Algernon goes "Bunburying" or Jack invents his rakish brother Earnest so that he may escape to the city. Another example is Miss Prism's sudden headache when the opportunity to go walking (and possibly indulge in some form of sexual activity) with Canon Chasuble presents itself.

Media Adaptations

- Universal International Films released a film adaptation of *The Importance of Being Earnest* in 1953. Directed by Anthony Asquith, the film stars Michael Redgrave as Jack/Earnest. It is available on video from Paramount.

Love and Passion

One of Wilde's satiric targets is romantic and sentimental love, which he ridicules by having the women fall in love with a man because of his name rather than more personal attributes. Wilde carries parody of romantic love to an extreme in the relationship between Algernon and Cecily, for she has fallen in love with him—and in fact charted their entire relationship—before ever meeting him. She writes of their love in her diary, noting the ups and downs of their affair, including authoring love letters to and from herself.

Culture Clash

The play's action is divided between the city and the country, London and the pastoral county of Hertfordshire. Traditionally, locations like these symbolize different attitudes toward life, contrasting, for example, the corruption of urban living with the simple bucolic pleasures of rural farm life. As Jack says, "when one is in town one amuses oneself. When one is in the country one amuses other people. It is excessively boring." Wilde's symbolism does not adhere rigidly to audience expectations, however. Though Jack is more sedate while in the country and more festive when in London, Cecily is far from the innocent she appears (and pretends to be around her guardian). Her handling of her "affair" with Algernon/Earnest shows her to be as competent in romance as any city woman. The trait is seen again when Gwendolen visits. During their tiff over just who gets Earnest (who they believe to be one man), Cecily holds her own and then some against her sophisticated city guest.

Topics for Further Study

- Wilde's play revolves around the necessity of telling lies in order to keep polite society polite. Is such dishonesty really necessary? What would the world be like if everyone were absolutely honest? What would happen to you if you were honest for one week?

- Many psychologists, sociologists, and literary scholars consider Oscar Wilde's trial as the moment which marks the birth of the modern homosexual identity. Read an account of Wilde's trial or his novel *The Portrait of Dorian Gray* and consider the social and aesthetic issues which surround sexual identity.

- In many ways, Wilde's play is a send up of gender roles and a travesty of romantic idealism. Are love and marriage really as simple—or complicated—as they seem in *Earnest?* How should men and women behave toward each other? What do people really want in relationships? What makes for a successful or unsuccessful marriage?

- In *Earnest*, people in the country behave—or at least, are expected to behave—differently from their counterparts in the city. Are the stereotypes of city and country life still with us? Identify those stereotypes and consider how population growth, shifting

demographics, and urbanization have affected the ways we think about rural and urban life.
- Critics have commented on the "triviality" of Wilde's play—that is, it's celebration of the superficial at the expense of earnest seriousness. As an advocate of the Aesthetic movement, though, Wilde might agree with those characters in *Earnest* who value form over content. Consider the ways Wilde's play critiques contemporary Victorian values.

Language and Meaning

Those familiar with semiotic theory (signs and symbols) will notice the ways various characters in the play obsess over the signifier. The best example is the desire of both Gwendolen and Cecily to love men named Earnest. They see something mystical in the processing of naming and assume some connection between the word (the signifier) and the person (the signified), that one who is named Earnest will naturally behave earnestly.

Freedom

Both Jack and Algernon struggle to remain free of the restrictions of Victorian convention. Jack does so by maintaining a double identity, being Jack in the country and Earnest in the city. Algernon achieves similar results by inventing an invalid named Bunbury who constantly requires his attentions. This similarity in Algernon and Jack's behavior also offers a clue to the men's true relationship as brothers (further duality is indicated by their respective attractions to very similar women, Gwendolen and Cecily).

Style

Romantic Comedy

Most commonly seen in Shakespeare's romance plays like *As You Like It* or *A Midsummer Night's Dream*, the plot of a typical romantic comedy involves an idealized pair of lovers who the circumstances of daily life or social convention seem destined to keep apart. Along the way, the lovers escape their troubles, at least for a while, entering an ideal world (like the Garden of Eden) where conflicts resolve and the lovers ultimately come together. The plots of such comedies contain pairs of characters and conclude happily, often exhibiting poetic justice, with the good rewarded and the evil punished.

While *The Importance of Being Earnest* certainly fits this description, it is a play that is appraised beyond simple romantic comedy. In fact, part of the play's wide and lasting appeal is that it so competently fits into any number of comedy genres, including comedies of manners, farces, and parodies.

Comedy of Manners

Generally set in sophisticated society, this type of intellectual comedy privileges witty dialogue over plot, though social intrigue involving the problems of lovers—faithful and unfaithful—can be complicated. The comedy arises from the critique of the fashions, manners, and behavior of elevated society. While often featuring standard characters such as fools, fops, conniving servants, and jealous husbands, the action itself is largely realistic. At least one character, like the audience, accurately comprehends the foolish nature of the people and their situations. In addition to Restoration Comedies like William Congreve's *The Way of the World*, other examples would be Goldsmith's *She Stoops to Conquer*, Sheridan's *School for Scandal*, and Noel Coward's *Private Lives*.

Farce

This type of low comedy relies on physical gags, coarse wit, and generally broad humor. Laughter arises as exaggerated characters, sometimes caricatures of social types, extricate themselves from improbable situations. Farce occasionally involves disguise or the confusion of gender roles. Algernon's indulgence with food and his short attention span qualify him as a farcical character, as does Miss Prism's bumbling mix-up with her novel and the infant Jack.

Parody

A work which, for comic or satiric effect, imitates another, familiar, usually serious work, mocking the recognizable trademarks of an individual author, style, or genre. Successful parody assumes an informed audience, with knowledge of the parodied target. For example, one of the most parodied works today is the "Mona Lisa" painting which shows up in cartoons, advertisements, and fine art. In *Earnest*, Wilde parodies, among other things, love at first sight by having his characters fall in love before they ever see each other.

Historical Context

As the nineteenth century drew to a close, England witnessed a cultural and artistic turn against the values of Queen Victoria's reign (1837-1901). These earlier virtues, such as self-help and respectability, were widely touted during the boom years of the 1860s and 1870s. However, people were less able to help themselves and raise their social standing in the late 1870s, when farming practices underwent a change which affected society as a whole.

Wheat-fields were converted to cattle pastures on a sweeping scale, and farmers suffered. While farmers were struggling, industrialists were profiting from their factories which employed workers at cheap wages. Factory owners and other businessmen formed the new middle class in England, and as they rose on the social ladder, they desired to imitate the aristocracy by owning houses in the countryside and becoming patrons of art.

As people began questioning the values of the mid-nineteenth century, artists responded in their own way by reacting against the mass-produced goods which were made possible by the Industrial Revolution and technological advances. Artists such as William Morris desired a return to simpler times when handmade furniture, for example, was valued for its craftsmanship. Morris despised the mass-produced objects which filled the Victorian home, fearing that traditional crafts such as woodworking and bookbinding would be lost in an era that overlooked the beauty of handmade objects in favor of high quantity. The term "Arts and Crafts," coined in 1888, refers to Morris's revival of traditional crafts, which he considered to be equal to any form of so-called "high art."

Morris argued that in earlier times, such as the Middle Ages (of which he held a decidedly romantic view), art was all around, in everyday life, in the form of beautifully worked tapestries, furniture, and books, which were not just admired as art objects but had a practical function as well.

Compare & Contrast

- **1800s:** Theatre is one of the most popular forms of mass entertainment. The number of theatres built in England doubles between 1850 and 1860, and on a given night in London alone, 150,000 people attend the theatre.

  Today: While theatre remains an important force in contemporary culture, many more people watch television and films.

- **1800s:** Women in England cannot vote or control their own property until a series of Married Women's Property Acts (1870-1908). Though the first college offering advanced education to women is founded in London in 1848, by the 1890s, women can take degrees at twelve British universities, and study, though not take degrees, at Oxford and Cambridge.

Today: British women, like their American counterparts, vote, control their own property, and have all the same legal rights as men, including the right to advanced degrees in education.

- **1800s:** During the Victorian period, travel by rail makes business and vacation travel possible. Trains bring city and country closer together, expediting mail service and supplying rural areas with London newspapers and magazines.

  Today: Few people in American travel by rail; most drive cars or fly.

- **1800s:** Britain has a far-flung imperial empire, with colonies around the globe.

  Today: Most of Britain's colonies have achieved their independence, though they continue to be affiliated with the former empire as members of the British Commonwealth.

Another way in which artists reacted against earlier Victorian values was by challenging the view that art had to be didactic or morally instructive. The leading critic of the time, John Ruskin, had earlier written that art's highest purpose was to instruct and enlighten. Ruskin was shocked when he saw a sketchy, impressionistic painting by James Abbot McNeill Whistler which had paint spattered on it; he claimed that Whistler had "flung a pot of paint in the public's face." Whistler sued Ruskin for libel, winning the case and bringing the debate over the purpose of art into the public.

Supporters of Whistler approved of "art for art's sake," meaning that paintings like Whistler's need not have a purpose other than to be aesthetically pleasing. Even if it was pleasing to see paint spattered on the canvas. The public could now decide for themselves what was "good" art; they did not need to rely on the views of critics like Ruskin to instruct them in the meaning of a painting.

This new movement in art came to be known as Aestheticism, as art could now be appreciated on purely aesthetic terms. Wilde followed Whistler as the chief spokesperson for the movement, writing and lecturing on the beauty of art for art's sake and became known for his own desire to have life imitate art, not the other way around. Aesthetes such as Wilde were mocked in the popular British magazine *Punch* as foppish, unrealistic individuals who strove to live up to the beauty of their home furnishings.

Critical Overview

Two major issues predominate much of *The Importance of Being Earnest's* criticism. First, while audiences from the play's opening have warmly received it, Wilde's contemporaries questioned its seeming amorality. Playwright George Bernard Shaw (*Major Barbara*), after seeing the original London production, attacked the play's "real degeneracy" in an article reprinted in *Oscar Wilde: A Collection of Critical Essays*. Shaw described Wilde's repartee as "hateful" and "sinister." A second and related concern arises about *Earnest's* dramatic structure, which exhibits elements of the farce, comedy of manners, and parody. Critics often disagree as to how the play should be categorized.

On the play's morality, critical opinion remains divided. In his book *Oscar Wilde*, Edouard Roditi, for example, believed that Wilde's comedy never rises above "the incomplete or the trivial." Because none of the characters see through the others or critique their values, Roditi believed the play lacks an ethical point of view. Eric Bentley, in *The Playwright As Thinker*, raised similar issues, concluding that because of its "ridiculous action," the play fails to "break . . . into bitter criticism" of serious issues.

For Otto Reinert, writing in *College English*, Wilde's comedy results in "an exposure both of hypocrisy and of the unnatural convention that necessitates hypocrisy." As a consequence, "bunburying," the reliance on white lies that keeps polite society polite, "gives the plot moral significance." For example, when Lady Bracknell criticizes Algernon for caring for his imaginary friend, Bunbury, who should decide "whether he was going to live or to die," she voices the conventional belief that "illness in others is always faked [and] . . . consequently sympathy with invalids is faked also."

Though Lady Bracknell respects convention, Reinert wrote, "she has no illusions about the reality her professed convention is supposed to conceal." She assumes that both Algernon and Bunbury are "bunburying," and her behavior "exposes the polite cynicism that negates all values save personal convenience and salon decorum."

Nor is Lady Bracknell immune from her own lapses in earnestness. Stating her disapproval of mercenary marriages, she admits, "When I married Lord Bracknell I had no fortune of any kind." That is, though she opposes marrying for money, she had no money when she married a wealthy lord. For her, according to Reinert, this position "is neither cynical nor funny. It represents . . . [a] compromise between practical hardheadedness and conventional morality."

Overall, the play does not endorse social dishonesty, for while the plot ridicules respectability, "it also repudiates Bunburyism." Wilde's use of "paradoxical morality" serves as a critique of "the problem of manners," for "Bunburying Algernon, in escaping the hypocrisy of convention, becomes a hypocrite himself by pretending to be somebody he is not." Wilde sees that Victorian respectability forces people to lead "double lives, one respectable, one frivolous, neither earnest."

The second critical issue concerns the play's categorization. Reinert unapologetically describes the play as a farce "that represents the reality that Victorian convention pretends to ignore." The characters themselves are not being ironic, *i.e.* saying one thing and meaning another. They actually mean what they say. For example, Algernon despairs of attending Lady Bracknell's dinner party because she will sit him beside "Mary Farquhar, who always flirts with her own husband." As Reinert wrote, "Algernon is indignant with a woman who spoils the fun of extramarital flirtation and who parades her virtue. He is shocked at convention. And his tone implies that he is elevating break of convention into a moral norm," that is, making the unconventional conventional.

Characters like Algernon, who resemble those in works by Alexander Pope (*The Rape of the Lock*) and Jonathan Swift (*Gulliver's Travels*), "derive their ideals for conduct from the actual practice of their societies, their standards are the standards of common corruption, they are literal-minded victims of their environments, realists with a vengeance."

For Richard Foster, writing in *College English*, Wilde's comedy works through parody, by transforming "stock comedic techniques, plot devices, and characters." Foster defended the play against charges that it is merely farce, because farce "depends for its effects upon extremely simplified characters tangling themselves up in incongruous situations," as in Shakespeare's *The Comedy of Errors* or Goldsmith's *She Stoops to Conquer*. Instead, "the comedy of *Earnest* subsists, for the most part, not in action or situation but in dialogue" which is too witty and intellectual "to be described simply as a farce."

Nor is *Earnest* actually a comedy of manners, according to Foster, though it does use verbal wit to expose and ridicule "the vanities, the hypocrisies, and the idleness of the upper classes." After all, a "comedy of manners is fundamentally realistic," requiring the audience to see the stage world as real or possible, if exaggerated. To assist in this recognition, some characters and the audience recognize the fools. In a comedy of manners, folly is recognized by some characters and the audience, while in *Earnest*, according to Rosemary Pountney in *The International Dictionary of Theatre*, Wilde creates "a world of deliberately reversed values" in which the wicked are charming and the good, boring.

Rather than a farce or comedy of manners, then, Foster saw Wilde using familiar plot devices and characters to satirize Victorian society. Jack's relationship with Gwendolen evidences a stock problem of lovers prevented from marriage by class differences. Wilde's solution: establishing the true patrimony of Jack, the railway station infant. Another commonplace of romantic literature is love at first sight, but in *Earnest*, Cecily has fallen in love with Algernon before first sight, solely because she believes his name to be Earnest. And while Algernon is cynical, there is evidence that his cynicism is superficial, for immediately on meeting Cecily, "Algernon is engaged to be married and reconciled to getting christened."

Cecily, seemingly sheltered and innocent, suggests it would be hypocritical for Algernon to actually be good while presenting to be wicked. "The moral of Wilde's parody: the rake is a fake, girlish innocence is the bait of a monstrous mantrap, the wages of sin in matrimony." What some critics identify as dramatic problems, then, are perceived by others as the play's strengths. "Nothing in the play," wrote Foster, "is quite what it seems. . . . The play's 'flaws'—the contrivances of plot, the convenience of its coincidences, and the neatness of its resolution—are," according to Foster, "of course, its whole point."

Sources

Beckson, Karl. "Oscar Wilde" in *Concise Dictionary of British Literary Biography*, Volume 4: *Victorian Writers, 1832-1890*, Gale, 1991, pp. 340-55.

Bentley, Eric. *The Playwright As Thinker*, Reynal & Hitchcock, 1946.

Foster, Richard. "Wilde As Parodist: A Second Look at 'The Importance of Being Earnest'" in *College English*, Vol. 18, no. 1, October, 1956, pp. 18-23.

Pountney, Rosemary. "The Importance of Being Earnest" in *The International Dictionary of Theatre*, Volume 1: *Plays*, edited by Mark Hawkins-Dady, St. James Press, 1992.

Reinert, Otto. "Satiric Strategy in 'The Importance of Being Earnest'" in *College English*, Vol. 18, no. 1, October, 1956, pp. 14-18.

Roditi, Edourd. *Oscar Wilde*, New Directions, 1986.

Further Reading

Beckson, Karl, Editor. *Oscar Wilde: The Critical Heritage*, Routlege, 1970.

> Focusing on the years 1881 to 1927, this book offers particular insight into Wilde's theatrical writings.

Briggs, Asa. *The Age of Improvement*, Longman, 1988.

> A readable, comprehensive history of the mid-Victorian years in England. Useful for understanding the nineteenth century generally, including social history.

Ellmann, Richard. *Oscar Wilde*, 1988.

> This is the standard literary biography of Wilde, providing a wealth of detail about his personal life as well as insight into the composition of his works.

Ellmann, Richard, Editor. *Oscar Wilde: A Collection of Critical Essays*, Prentice-Hall, 1969.

> Most helpful for exploring the thinking about Wilde by his contemporaries such as W. B. Yeats and George Bernard Shaw.

Hobsbawm, Eric. *The Age of Capital, 1848-1875*, McKay, 1975.

Although this history concentrates on the middle of the nineteenth century, Hobsbawm usefully situates the roots of social trends that would influence British society in the 1890s.

Holland, Vyvyan B. *Oscar Wilde: A Pictorial Biography*, Viking, 1961.

Holland is Wilde's son. While this book contains a brief biography, the highlights are the fine photographs of Wilde and many of the people in his life, public and private.

Lightning Source UK Ltd.
Milton Keynes UK
UKHW021610300419
341861UK00011B/754/P